# Cheerleading

# RULES

This book could not have been written without the help and creative talents of the cheerleading squad at *Wallace County High School* in Sharon Springs, Kansas: **Lexie Bellamy, Tammy Bolen, Evany Davis, Michelle Ford, Sarah Hill, Tessa Howard, Morgan Unruh,** and **Danielle Van Laeys.**

The cheer positions and stunts in this book were modeled by the cheer squad of *Sammamish High School* in Bellevue, Washington: Katie McGarity, Jill Beaudry, Anastasia Beiting, Amy Crawford, Jennifer Fritz, Amanda Kowalski, Michelle Magnotti, Briana Pelton, Kiki Rizki, Reagan Sutton, Cherisse Swann, Erica Wilkerson, Helen Wong, and Ronda Herd. This amazing group of athletes is coached by Kristine Scholl, without whom this book would not have been possible.

**becker&mayer!**

© 2005 by becker&mayer! LLC
Published by becker&mayer! LLC, Bellevue, WA 98004
www.beckermayer.com
If you have questions or comments about this
product, send e-mail to infobm@beckermayer.com.
All rights reserved.

Written by Eva L. Siebert
Book designed by Karrie Lee and Scott Westgard
Photography by Keith Megay
Edited by Betsy Henry Pringle
Production management by Jennifer Marx
All rights reserved.
Printed in the United States of America
10 9 8 7 6 5 4 3 2 1
ISBN: 1-932855-36-X
05060

# Table of
# CONTENTS

# Stand Up and Cheer!

## DID YOU KNOW:

 **50%** OF ALL CHEERLEADERS ARE ALSO VARSITY ATHLETES.

 **85%** OF ALL CHEERLEADERS HAVE A "B" AVERAGE OR BETTER.

 **65%** OF ALL CHEERLEADERS PARTICIPATE IN OTHER EXTRACURRICULAR ACTIVITIES.

As these facts show, cheerleaders are some of the most athletic, intelligent, and involved students in a school. Is this the kind of person you would like to be? **Then *Cheerleading Rules!* is the right book for you.**

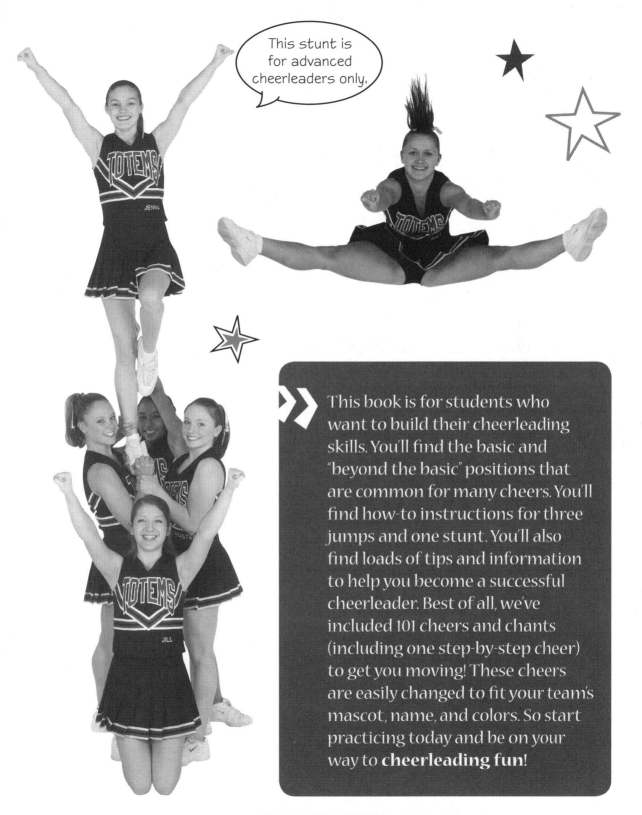

This book is for students who want to build their cheerleading skills. You'll find the basic and "beyond the basic" positions that are common for many cheers. You'll find how-to instructions for three jumps and one stunt. You'll also find loads of tips and information to help you become a successful cheerleader. Best of all, we've included 101 cheers and chants (including one step-by-step cheer) to get you moving! These cheers are easily changed to fit your team's mascot, name, and colors. So start practicing today and be on your way to **cheerleading fun!**

# What Every **Cheerleader** Should KNOW

This stunt is for advanced cheerleaders only.

"I love to cheer because I get to hang out with all my friends and have super fun on the bus rides!"
-Lexie Bellamy

You already know that cheerleading is awesome! But you might not be aware of all the benefits of being a cheerleader. One of the most important is that you have a squad where you belong and are part of a group. As a cheerleader, you meet new friends, both at your school and from other squads. You also stay healthy and get plenty (and we mean PLENTY!) of exercise.

Cheerleaders build trust, boost team spirit, and show leadership. Over time, cheerleaders become more graceful, overcome shyness, learn responsibility, and develop greater confidence and self-esteem. Cheerleaders are enthusiastic and cooperative. All of these traits are part of becoming a better "you"!

# BEFORE YOU BEGIN

Every sport requires conditioning. Cheerleading is no different! Warming up and cooling down before and after every practice and game are vital parts of any routine.

## ❯ WARM UP

Warming up consists mainly of stretching, especially the leg muscles. One easy way to do this is to sit on the floor with your legs spread apart in front of you in the "V" shape. Reach your right hand to touch your left toes, and then repeat going the other direction; reach your left hand to touch your right toes. Other simple exercises like toe-touches, windmills, and jumping jacks will also help warm up your muscles.

## ❯❯ COOL DOWN

Cooling down is important because it brings your heart rate back to a normal speed. Walking around the gym or practice area at a slow to normal pace is a good way to cool down. When your heart rate is back to normal, repeat the stretches you did earlier.

### RAH RAH SAFETY

MAKING EVERY WORKOUT SAFE SHOULD BE A GOAL FOR YOU, YOUR PARENTS, AND YOUR CHEER COACH. (AFTER ALL, YOU WANT TO BE JUMPING AND KICKING, NOT SITTING ON THE BENCH WITH SORE MUSCLES, RIGHT?) SO, WARM UP AND SEE THE BENEFITS PILE UP!

## Benefits of Conditioning

- No sore muscles
- Better flexibility
- Increased strength—and that means better jumps and higher kicks!

# Tips for Being in
## TOP CHEER CONDITION

**Warm**

- Stretch and strengthen your muscles and joints by warming up before the activity.

- Drink plenty of water.

- Get involved in an aerobic exercise like swimming, walking, jogging, jumping rope, or bicycling.

- Work out your upper body with push-ups.

- Strengthen your abdominal muscles with crunches.

- Power up and tone your lower body with squats and step-ups.

- Cool down following the activity. **Cool**

## DID YOU KNOW:

CHEERLEADING IS A GROWING SPORT THAT IS SPREADING ACROSS THE COUNTRY. MANY STATE ATHLETIC ASSOCIATIONS NOW RECOGNIZE IT AS AN OFFICIAL SPORT. THAT MEANS THAT CHEERLEADERS ARE STUDENT ATHLETES, JUST LIKE BASKETBALL, FOOTBALL, AND VOLLEYBALL PLAYERS.

# *Basic Cheer* POSITIONS

All cheerleaders learn these basic positions. Practice them in front of a mirror and with your friends. Stand straight and tall, with your head held high. Don't forget to smile!

**T**

**GO MOTION**

**HIP HIGH V**

**HANDS ON HIPS**

## HIGH V

## LOW V

## LUNGE

## TOUCHDOWN

**LEFT K**

**RIGHT K**

**LIBERTY**

**DOUBLE DAGGERS**

# *Beyond the* BASICS

Learning these advanced cheer positions will add variety to your routines!

## BOW AND ARROW 1

## BOW AND ARROW 2

## BROKEN HIGH V

## BROKEN LOW V

## LEFT CROSS LOW V

## RIGHT CROSS LOW V

## MUSCLE MAN

## TABLETOP

## LOW SIDE TOUCHDOWN

## HALF-HIDDEN TOUCHDOWN

## RAISE THE ROOF

## LIBERTY PUNCH

## KARATE KICK

## KARATE PUNCH

## THE CARROT

## HOOP

## LEFT CORNER

## RIGHT CORNER

## CLEAN

## BROKEN ARM T

## BLADE HALF T

## FRONT X

## HALF-HIDDEN HIGH V

## HALF HIGH V

# Tips for **SUCCESS**

- When performing in front of a crowd, always maintain eye contact with the crowd and smile, smile, smile!

- Use a clear, strong voice and sharp motions.

- Encourage the crowd to get involved in the cheers. Do this by having them repeat a part of the cheer or by using signs. Crowd participation will, in turn, affect the team!

- Always be positive and display good sportsmanship.

- Rotate your cheers—don't get stuck in a rut!

- Share new ideas for cheers with your squad.

- Most of all, show your excitement and have FUN!

## DID YOU KNOW:

CHEERLEADING ENCOURAGES STUDENTS TO BE POSITIVE ROLE MODELS, DEVELOP LEADERSHIP SKILLS, INCREASE THEIR PHYSICAL WELLNESS, AND HAVE GREATER CONFIDENCE AND SELF-ESTEEM. AND WHEN YOU BECOME A CHEERLEADER, YOU DEVELOP FRIENDSHIPS AND SKILLS THAT WILL LAST A LIFETIME!

# Step-by-Step
# CHEER

Now that you know the moves, follow the steps on the following two pages to perform the "Stand Up!" cheer that's on page 62.

Substitute your team name and school letters. The cheer is repeated for each letter (W! C! H! S!). On the last round of the cheer, yell your team's letters all together (WCHS!).

Work on getting the moves to flow smoothly together like a dance!

# STEP 1

[motion: HiGH V]

Yell "CATS" (or your team)
Yell "CATS" (or your team)
Yell "CATS" (or your team)
Yell "CATS" (or your team)
Yell "CATS" (or your team)

# STEP 2

[motion: HALF-HiDDEN HiGH V,
RiGHT CROSS LOW V]

pause
pause
pause
pause
pause

# STEP 5

[motion: HALF TOUCHDOWN]

Yell "W" (school's 1st letter)
Yell "C" (school's 2nd letter)
Yell "H" (school's 3rd letter)
Yell "S" (school's 4th letter)
Yell "WCHS" (school's letters)

# STEP 6

[motion: SiNGLE DAGGER]

pause
pause
pause
pause
pause

## STEP 3

[motion: HALF HIGH V]

Yell "Stand Up!"
Yell "Stand Up!"
Yell "Stand Up!"
Yell "Stand Up!"
Yell "Stand Up!"

## STEP 4

[motion: CLEAN]

Yell "Let's Go!"
Yell "Let's Go!"
Yell "Let's Go!"
Yell "Let's Go!"
Yell "Let's Go!"

## STEP 7

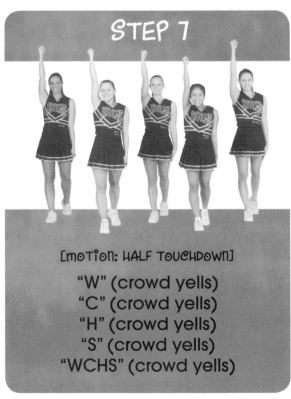

[motion: HALF TOUCHDOWN]

"W" (crowd yells)
"C" (crowd yells)
"H" (crowd yells)
"S" (crowd yells)
"WCHS" (crowd yells)

## STEP 8

[motion: GO MOTION]

clap
clap
clap
clap
clap

# Jump Up and CHEER

Jumping is an important part of cheerleading. Precise jumps are part of what the crowd notices about squads. You can become a champion jumper by practicing and by working on becoming stronger. An easy first step for beginners is to jump on a trampoline at home. This gives you the feel of "hang time" in the air and allows you time to perfect the motions. Once you are comfortable with the motions, move to the ground and practice, practice, practice!

Be sure to use the full range of motions with your arms and always land on the balls of your feet, never flat-footed. Also, remember to have your knees bent on the landing. Experiment with your own moves and, most of all, have fun!

# The FOUR PARTS to Every Jump:

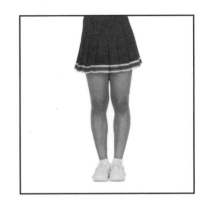

**1. Preparation:** Begin with your feet together and with your weight on the balls of your feet. Your arms will be in a High V.

**2. Lift:** This is where the practice comes in. You are trying to get your arms and feet to work together to get the perfect timing for height. Remember to use the full range of motion as you circle your arms. Keep your head up and eyes forward.

**3. Hang Time:** This is the peak of your jump. Try to hold this position for as long as possible! Again, keep your head up and eyes forward.

**4. Landing:** Bring your feet together. Remember to land on the balls of your feet, and have your knees slightly bent.

# The **PRETZEL**

**1.** Start with your feet together and your arms by your sides.

**2.** With one smooth motion, hit a High V with your arms as you rise onto your toes.

**3.** Get ready to jump by circling your arms in front of you and bending your legs.

**4.** Jump off the ground as high as you can jump. Hit a T or High V position with your arms while you bend one leg in front of you and the other behind. Both legs should be pointed to the side. Keep your toes pointed.

**5.** Land with your feet together and your arms at your sides.

# The "C"

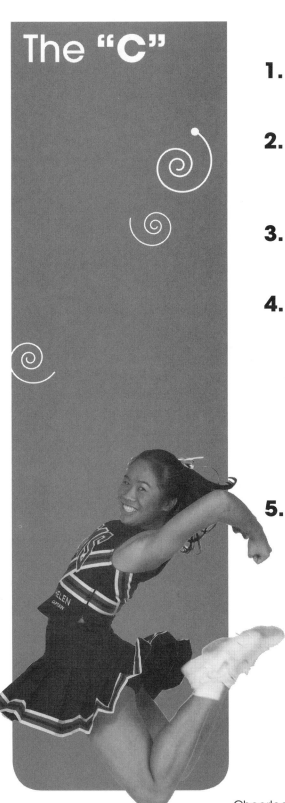

**1.** Start with you feet together and your arms by your sides.

**2.** With one smooth motion, hit a High V with your arms and rise onto your toes.

**3.** Circle your arms in front of your body as you bend your knees.

**4.** As you jump, tuck both legs slightly behind you and to the left. Your arms are bent at the elbows, with your right arm coming over your head and your left arm pulled to the left. Your arms and legs are forming the letter "C."

**5.** Land with your feet together and your arms at your sides.

# The **HERKEY**

**1.** Start with your feet together and your arms by your sides.

**2.** With one smooth motion, hit a High V with your arms as you rise onto your toes.

**3.** Circle your arms in front of your body as you bend your knees.

**4.** When you jump, kick one leg forward and level to your waist. Bend the other leg behind and to the side. Your arms can be in a High V, T, or reaching toward the front.

**5.** Land with your feet together and your arms at your sides.

# Stunning STUNTS

# There are three positions in every STUNT:
## the **Bases**, the ^Flyer, and the **Spotter**.

**FLYER:** The Flyer is the person who is lifted or steps up in the stunt. You might want to choose your lightest teammate to be the Flyer.

**SPOTTER:** The Spotter stands behind the stunt to secure the Flyer and to assist with the catch and dismount. Since the Flyer is often lifted, you might want to choose one of the taller cheerleaders on the squad to be the Spotter.

**BASES:** Bases are the people on the bottom of a stunt with their feet on the floor. The bases provide support for the Flyer.

Flyer

Spotter

Base

This stunt is for advanced cheerleaders only.

# Double-Based **Thigh Stand**

HAVE FUN TRYING THiS EASY STUNT WiTH YOUR FRiENDS! iT TAKES:

> 1 FLYER
> 1 SPOTTER
> 2 BASES

Read the instructions on the following pages carefully before you try this stunt, and make sure every girl knows the responsibility of her position.

## Safety Guidelines:
(Check with your school's cheer coach for a complete list of safety guidelines)

- ○ Have a knowledgeable coach or trained instructor present at all times.
- ● All cheerleaders should receive proper training before attempting any jumps or stunts.
- ○ Check with your school or organization to find out which stunts are legal for your squad to perform.
- ● All squad members should be taught proper spotting techniques.
- ○ Spotters must be used on all stunts.
- ● Practice in a suitable location and away from noise and distractions.
- ○ Remove jewelry and loose clothing when cheering and practicing.
- ● Hair should be fixed so that it is out of the face and will not cause a hazard when stunting.
- ○ Be sure you're on a good surface, such as a cheerleading mat or grass.

**1.** Begin with the **Bases** in a lunge, facing each other. Be sure the two **Bases'** inside feet are one behind the other.

The **Flyer** has her arms on the Bases' shoulders, so she can push herself up.

The **Spotter** has her hands securely on the Flyer's waist.

Flyer

Spotter

Base

Base

**3.** The **Flyer** then places her left foot in the pocket of the lunge on the left Base. The **Flyer** pushes on the Bases' shoulders to propel herself up into a full stand. When she is completely balanced, the **Flyer** makes a High V.

Both **Bases** now are holding the Flyer's feet and securing her behind her knees.

The **Spotter** still has hold of the Flyer's waist.

**2.** Beginning with the Base on the right, the **Flyer** lifts her right foot to fit securely in the pocket of the lunge.

The **Base** holds the Flyer's foot with one hand and secures her knee with the other hand.

The **Spotter** still has hold of the Flyer's waist.

**4.** To dismount, the **Flyer** brings her arms down and the **Bases** take hold of her hands with their outside arms. The **Flyer** then "hops" forward off the lunge of her Bases.

As each **Base** releases her hold on the Flyer's knees, that hand goes up and "catches" the Flyer under her extended arms.

The **Spotter** still has hold of the Flyer's waist.

# 101 Awesome

# CHEERS

# Key

## WCHS
Your school initials

---

## ( )
repeated by the fans

---

## [ ]
instructions for the fans

---

## WILDCATS/CATS
Your team mascot

---

## BEARS
The team you are playing

---

## BLUE & WHITE
Your school colors

---

## CLAP

---

## STOMP

# *Football* CHEERS

# Football Offense

### TOUCHDOWN
T-O-U-C-H down
 down

### SCORE
Score, Wildcats, score
6 points more

### DO IT AGAIN
Wildcats do it again
Work together for a
first and ten

"I love cheerleading. I think it's the best sport, and I enjoy learning new cheers and stunts. It is a great way to meet and become friends with people."
-Michelle Ford

# FIRST AND TEN/WIN

First and ten
Do it again
Let's win

# FIRST AND TEN

First and ten
Do it again
Go, fight, win

# MOVE IT

M-O-V-E I-T
Move it
Move it

# TOUCHDOWN/LET'S WIN

Touch D-O-W-N
Touchdown, let's win

"Cheerleading is so fun and exciting because it gives you a chance to lead your crowd in yelling for your team. What also makes it fun is the rest of the girls on the squad. With our squad of eight girls, it's like I have seven best friends that I do everything with!"
-Tammy Bolen

## SCORE 6 MORE

Touchdown, touchdown
Score 6 more

## TOUCHDOWN/WILDCATS

Touchdown, Wildcats
Score 6 more

## PUSH THROUGH

Push through, push through
Push through that line

# Football Defense

### END CENTER TACKLE GUARD

End, center, tackle, guard
Guard your man and
Guard him hard

### ATTACK

Attack, attack
Sack that quarterback

### PUSH 'EM BACK

Push 'em back
Push 'em back
Waaay back

### HOLD THAT LINE

H  O
L-D
Hold that line

# GO GET 'EM

Go, go get 'em
They'll never know what hit 'em

# HOLD THAT LINE

Hold that line
Hold that line

# DEFENSE, GET THAT BALL

Defense, get that ball—GO
Defense, get that ball—FIGHT
Defense, get that ball—WIN
Go, fight, win

# BRING YOU DOWN

Listen now, gonna bring you down
Gonna put you flat
and that is that

"Cheerleading has helped me make a lot of new friends and learn a lot about them and cheering. My favorite thing is being able to be with my cheer friends at pre-game parties!"
-Tessa Howard

# DEFENSE, HOLD 'EM

Defense, hold 'em
Hold that line

# HOLD 'EM

Hold 'em, hold 'em, Cats
Hold that line

# CATS, LET'S GO

Cats, let's go
Defense, take that ball away

# DEFENSE, GET TOUGH

Defense
Get tough, get tough
Defense, get tough

# Basketball

# CHEERS

# Basketball Sink it (for Free Throws)

## SINK IT 1
S-I-N-K Sink that ball
S-I-N-K Sink that ball

## SINK IT 2
S-W-I-S-H Swish that ball
Swish it, hey

## SINK IT 3
Sink it, sink it, sink it 👏👏 let's go

## SINK IT 4
See that basket, see that rim
Come on Nathan (player's name), put it in

## SINK IT 5
S-I-N-K I-T Sink it 👏👏 sink it 👏👏
S-I-N-K I-T, Sink it

## SINK IT 6
P-U-T I-T I-N, Put it in
P-U-T I-T I-N, Put it in

## SINK IT 7
Put it through the rim
The point will help us win

# Basketball Rebound (for Free Throws)

## REBOUND 1

R-E-B-O-U-N-D

Hey Cats, rebound

## REBOUND 2

Cats on the rebound, go, go
Cats on the rebound, go!

## REBOUND 3

Hey Cats, rebound!

## REBOUND 4

Rebound, rebound
Rebound, hey
Wildcats, get that ball, hey!

## REBOUND 5

Jump, jump, get it, get it
Rebound that ball
Jump, jump, get it, get it
Rebound that ball

# Basketball Offense

## TO THE HOOP

Take it to the hoop

Score 2 more

## SHOOT FOR 2

Swish that ball and shoot for 2

## TWO OR THREE

2 or 3, how 'bout it, 2 or 3

## WE WANT TWO

2, 2, 2, we want 2

## SHOOT IT THROUGH

Shoot it through

Shoot it through

Shoot it through for 2

## WORK IT IN

Set it up work it in

Set it up, work it in, let's win

## MOVE IT

M-O-V-E I-T, move it move it

# SET IT UP

Set it up, work it in
That's the way the Wildcats win

# JUMP BALL

Jump ball, jump ball
Get it, get it, go, go

# JUMP UP

Jump up
Move that ball down the court
We want 2

# SET IT UP TWO POINTS

Set it up 2 points 👏👏👏

# THROUGH THE HOOP

Take it down and put it through the hoop, 2
The hoop, 2

# BASKET BASKET

Basket, basket, 2 points, WCHS score 2 points

# BASKET

Basket, basket, score 2 more

# Basketball Defense

## FIGHT HARD

Fight hard, hey, let's go
Say fight hard, hey, let's go

## D-D-DEFENSE

D-D-Defense
Get, get, get that ball

## HUSTLE

H-U-S 👏👏 T-L-E 👏👏
H-U-S-T-L-E
Hustle, hustle for a victory

## HUSTLE HUSTLE

Hustle, hustle, go, go
Hustle, hustle, go

# NEVER GIVE IN

Never give in, hustle to the very end

# DEFENSE ATTACK

Defense attack, get it
Get that ball back

# ATTACK 'EM

A-T-T-A-C-K Attack 'em, big D

# HANDS UP

Hands up, defense, hands up

# TAKE, TAKE, TAKE IT AWAY

Take, take, take it away
Break, break, break it away
Take it away, break it away
Go, fight, win!

"Cheerleading is a fun sport, but it also takes
practice and dedication. Be sure you are always
careful in stunts, and don't forget a smile."
-Danielle Van Laeys

# General CHANTS

# GO BIG BLUE

Go Big Blue 👏👏 Go Big Blue 👏👏
(keep repeating)

# WILDCATS

Wildcats 👏👏 Wildcats 👏👏
(keep repeating)

# GO, FIGHT, WIN TONIGHT

Go, fight, win tonight
Boogie down all right, all right

# ROCK ON

Keep that spirit strong
Rock, rock on

## BEAT, DEFEAT

Beat, defeat, no doubt

## COME ON, LET'S GO

Come on, come on, let's go
Wildcats, let's go

## OUR SPIRIT IS THE BEST

Absolutely, positively, Y-E-S
Our spirit is the best

## FIRE UP, UP

Fire up, up, everybody fire up

## F-I-R-E UP

F-I-R-E up, fire up

# FIRECRACKER, FIRECRACKER

Firecracker, firecracker
Turn up the heat
Cats are the team that
Can't be beat!
Go Cats!

# GO, WILDCATS, GO

G-O
Go, Wildcats, go

# YOU CAN DO IT

You can do it
If you try
V-I-C-T-O-R-Y

"I love to cheer because it gives me a chance to yell and scream with my friends. I like to be able to support the team."
-Evany Davis

# VICTORY

V, V-I, V-I-C-T-O-R-Y
Hold the V, dot the I
Rock that C-T-O-R-Y

# BEAT THE BEARS

B E A T
Come on, Wildcats
Beat the Bears
(mascot of the team
you are playing)

# GO GET 'EM

Blue and White
Go get 'em and
Fight, fight, fight

## LET'S GO BLUE

Let's go Blue, let's go White,
Blue 👏 White 👏

## GO BLUE, GO WHITE

Go Blue 👏👏 go White 👏👏
Go Blue, go White, WCHS

## GO BLUE

Go Blue, go White, beat those Bears

## SUPERSPIRIT

Y, because our pride is E, electrifying
S, for superspirit, Y-E-S

## HEY, HEY

Hey, hey, here we go
WCHS 👏👏 Wildcats 👏👏

# THAT'S IT, THAT'S RIGHT

Go, go, fight, fight, yeah
That's it, that's right

# LET'S GO

W-I-L-D C-A-T-S, let's go

# UP, UP ON YOUR FEET

Up, up, on your feet
Wildcats, Wildcats can't be beat

# GET OUT OF YOUR SEAT

Get up, get up, out of your seat
And listen to the rhythm of the Wildcat beat
Go 👟👋👟👋 go Big Blue,
👟👋👟👋 go Big Blue

"Cheering is fun, because you get to be with girls that are like you, and you can be as weird as you want to be."
-Sarah Hill

# CATS, LET'S HEAR IT

Cats, let's hear it
Yell and raise some spirit
Go Big Blue go, Blue, go

# WE GOT SPIRIT

S-P (S-P), I-R (I-R), I-T( I-T)
We got spirit we got soul

# WILDCATS IN THE HOUSE

Wildcats in the house
Yell "Go Big Blue" (GO BIG BLUE!)

# LET'S GO, CATS

Yell it, louder now
Let's go, Cats

# SPIRIT, SPIRIT LET'S HEAR IT

S-P-I R-I-T
Spirit, spirit let's hear it

## STOMP YOUR FEET

Stomp  your feet
Wildcats can't be beat

## LEAN TO THE LEFT

Lean to the left
(everyone leans left)
Lean to the right
(everyone leans right)
Stand up (everyone stands)
Sit down (everyone sits)
Fight, fight, fight!

## FOR THE BLUE, BLUE, BLUE

For the Blue, Blue, Blue
(left half of the stands yells)
For the White, White, White
(right half of the stands yells)
For the Blue (left half)
For the White (right half)
Let's fight (all yell together)

# ROWDIE

R-O-W-D-I-E that's the way we spell

Rowdie, rowdie, hey, hey, rowdie

# RED HOT

Our team is red hot

Our team is red hot

Our team is R-E-D, spell it out for us

H-O-T, now the rest of it

R-E-D Red H-O-T Hot

Red hot team that can't be stopped!

# GIVE IT ALL YOU GOT

Give it all you got

Give it all you got

Whew, whew, baby, baby

Give it all you got!

# CHEERS

## WAY OUT WEST

Way out West where the Wildcats roam
A little, bitty town we call our home
You may think that our team is small
But the bigger they are
The harder they fall
Bum, bum, bum, bu dum, bum, bum, bum
Bu dum, bum bum bum bu dum
Go Big Blue

## GO, CATS, GO

1,2,3,4, Come on, come on yell
"Go, Cats, go" (go, Cats, go)
1,2,3,4, Come on, come on yell
"Beat those Bears" (Beat those Bears)
Come on, come on yell "Go, Cats, go"
"Beat those Bears" (everyone yells together)

## CATS, STAND UP

Cats, stand up, let's go yell "W" (W!)
Cats, stand up, let's go yell "C" (C!)
Cats, stand up, let's go yell "H" (H!)
Cats, stand up, let's go yell "S" (S!)
Cats, stand up, let's go yell "WCHS" (WCHS!)

## HOW DO YOU FEEL

8th grade, 8th grade, how do you feel?
We feel good, oh we feel so good, uh!
(all 8th graders stand up and yell)
7th grade, 7th grade, how do you feel?
We feel good, oh we feel so good, uh!
(all 7th graders stand up and yell)

(REPEAT FOR EACH CLASS IN ATTENDANCE)